Library of Congress Cataloging-in-Publication Data

Watts, Barrie.
   Dragonfly/Barrie Watts.
     p. cm.–(Stopwatch books)
   Includes index.
   Summary: Photographs, drawings, and text depict how a dragonfly
hatches from a tiny egg, lives underwater as a nymph, and finally
emerges fully grown to fly away.
   1. Dragonflies–Juvenile literature. [1. Dragonflies.]
I. Title. II. Series.
QL520.W38 1988
595.7'33–dc19
                                       88-18412
ISBN 0-382-09800-5.   CIP
ISBN 0-382-09799-8 (lib. bdg.).   AC

First published by A & C Black (Publishers) Limited
35 Bedford Row, London WC1R 4JH

Copyright © 1988 Barrie Watts

Adapted and published in the United States in 1989
by Silver Burdett Press, Englewood Cliffs, New Jersey
U.S. project editor: Nancy Furstinger

Acknowledgments
The artwork is by Helen Senior
The publishers would like to thank Jennifer Coldrey for her help and advice.

Dragonfly

Barrie Watts

Silver Burdett Press • Englewood Cliffs, New Jersey

Here is a dragonfly.

Have you ever seen an insect like this one?
It is a dragonfly. You can watch dragonflies dart
and hover over ponds and rivers.

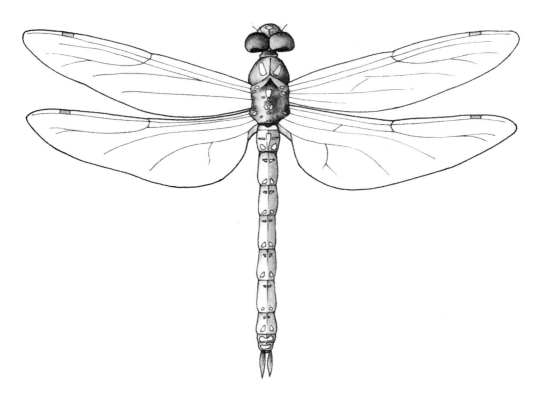

This book will tell you how a dragonfly hatches from
a tiny egg.

The female dragonfly lays her eggs.

In summer, the male and female dragonflies mate.

The male dragonfly has claws at the end of his body. He holds the female by her neck. The female bends her body toward the male.

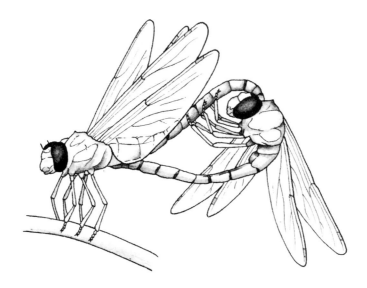

After a few minutes they have finished mating. The female flies away to find a wet place to lay her eggs.

Look at the big photograph. The dragonfly has found a damp log by a pond. She uses a tube at the end of her body to push her eggs into the log, one by one.

The eggs hatch.

Look at the photograph. The eggs are long and thin. This photograph has been enlarged to make the eggs look very big. In real life, each egg is as small as the top of a pin.

Through the winter, the eggs stay safe in the damp log. In spring, tiny creatures push their way out of the eggs. They are called nymphs.

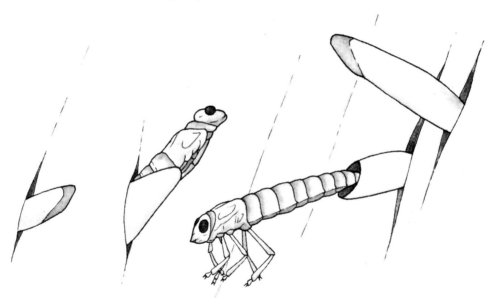

As soon as the nymphs have hatched, they hop in the pond.

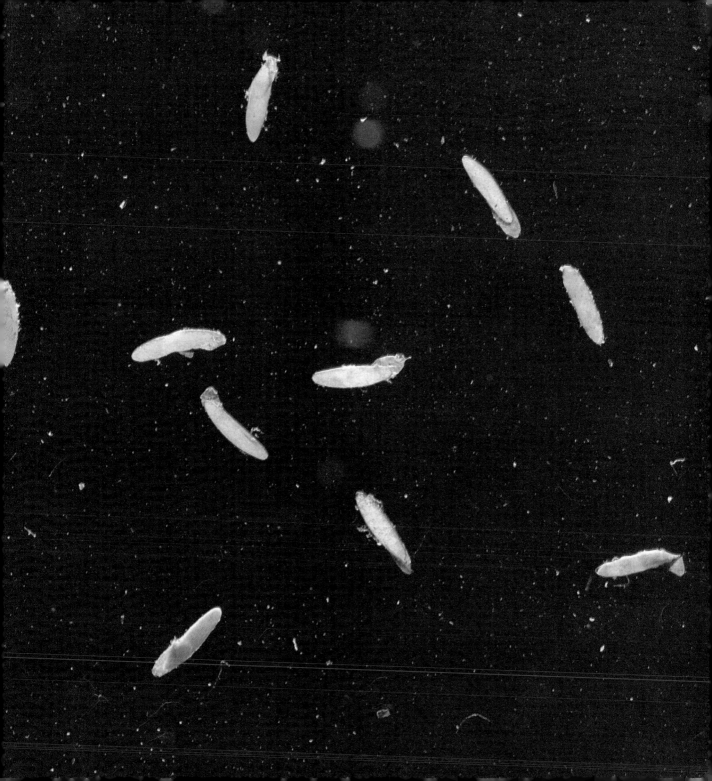

The young dragonfly gets bigger.

The dragonfly nymph lives under the water. It grows bigger and fatter. Soon its skin gets tight and starts to split, like this.

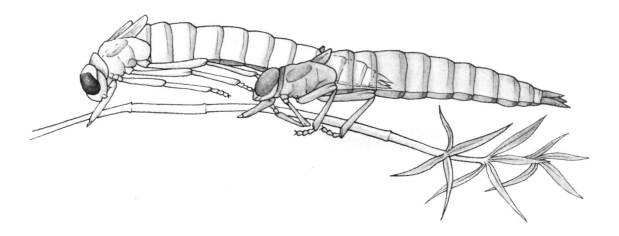

The nymph pushes its way out of the skin, head first. It will change its skin twelve times before it is fully grown.

Look at the photograph. After the nymph has changed its skin four times, tiny wing cases appear on its back. The nymph cannot use its wings yet.

The young dragonfly is hungry.

Look at the big photograph. This nymph's head is shown up close.

The nymph has big eyes to spot its food. It has a long bottom lip called a mask. Most of the time, the mask stays folded under the nymph's head. When a tadpole or small fish comes near, the mask grabs the animal and brings it to the nymph's mouth, like this.

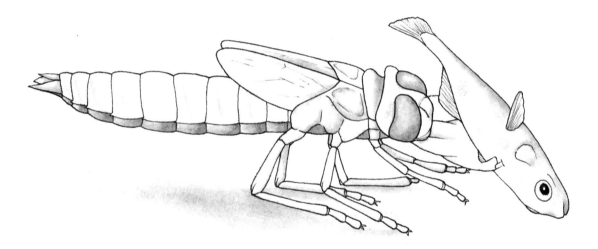

The nymph eats most small pond animals, and it will even eat other nymphs.

The young dragonfly climbs out of the water.

After two or three years, the dragonfly nymph is fully grown and it stops eating. It is now as big as a match.

One night in late summer, the nymph finds a tall reed sticking out of the water. Quickly it climbs the reed.

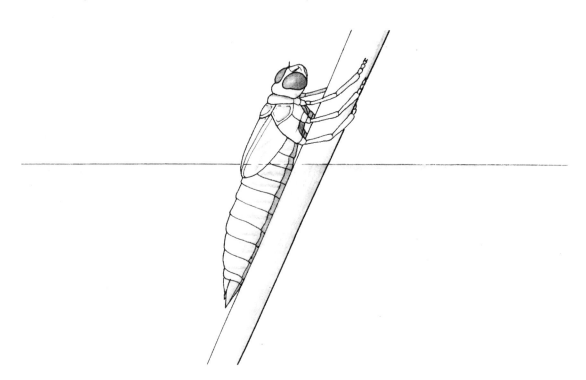

When the dragonfly nymph is right above the water, it stops. It digs its feet into the reed. Then it sways from side to side to make sure it has a firm hold.

The adult dragonfly begins to appear.

The nymph rests on the reed for fifteen minutes.
Then, suddenly, the skin behind its head starts to split.
The bright green adult dragonfly begins to show.

First the dragonfly pulls its head out. Slowly it pushes
and wriggles the front end of its body out of the old skin.

Look at the big photograph. The dragonfly has pulled out
its front legs. They are soft and weak.

The dragonfly rests.

When the dragonfly has pulled out all of its legs, it rests for about half an hour.

The dragonfly hangs upside down. It is held up by the end of its body, which is still inside the old skin. Its legs dry and get stronger.

When the dragonfly is ready, it suddenly jerks back up. Then it grips the old skin tightly and pulls the rest of its body out.

The dragonfly is soft and wet.

The dragonfly is now right side up. It holds on to the old skin and waits for its body to dry. Its four wings are tiny and crumpled.

The dragonfly begins to pump blood into its wings. This makes them get bigger.

After five minutes the wings are three times bigger. They are still soft and damp.

The dragonfly dries its wings.

After fifteen minutes, the dragonfly's wings are the right size. But they are still soft and the dragonfly cannot fly.

The wings have little lines all over them. They are called veins. The veins carry blood to the wings.

Look at the big photograph. After four hours, the dragonfly's wings are dry and strong, and its body has become straight and hard.

The dragonfly flies away.

Another hour goes by, and the dragonfly spreads its wings. When daylight comes, it is ready to fly away from the pond.

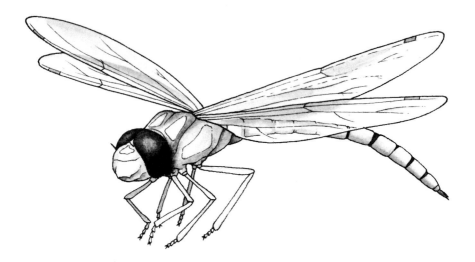

The dragonfly eats small insects, like flies.
It catches them in the air. Dragonflies can fly very fast.
They only fly when the weather is warm.

After about a week this dragonfly will look for a mate.
What do you think will happen then?

Do you remember how the dragonfly hatched from the egg?
See if you can tell the story in your own words. You can use
these pictures to help you.

Index

This index will help you to find some of the important words in the book

If there is a pond or river near where you live, you could look for some old dragonfly skins, attached to reeds.